# Successful Guide for Connecting Foster and Adoptive Families

*Learn how to connect with your foster and adoptive teen by applying 15 helpful tips given by former foster and adoptive teens.*

Teenagers can be a mystery to say the least. Teens that have been through the foster care system can be even more of a challenge as they put the past behind them, and move forward with their lives. Often they must move on while living with someone who is not their biological family. In this setting they can very difficult to connect with. They need a great community of people to guide them to success and it starts with amazing parents.

In this revolutionary Itty Bitty Book, James Poindexter III,CC gives you 15 tips with explanations on how to connect with your teen and guide them to success.

These tips are handpicked success tips given by former foster teens who have lived through the process and learned the do's and don'ts. Tips like:

- The Same Key Doesn't Fit Every Lock
- Look, Listen & Apply
- Give Us An Outlet

**WISH IT WAS WRITTEN SOONER**
**"Your Amazing Itty-Bitty Foster & Adoptive Parent Guide:** 15 Key Steps to Successfully Connect with Your Foster or Adopted Teen", is a must read. James A. Poindexter, III, CC, has done an amazing job in writing this book. First, I wish it had been written years ago. So many lives would have been saved and so much understanding would have been given for those who genuinely seek to make a difference in the foster and adoptive care children's lives.

This book is extremely powerful, yet the simplicity of the truths reveals a solid bridge of hope, insight, tools and confidence there is light at the end of the tunnel for anyone undertaking this journey.

There is no doubt in my mind this book should be a mandatory read for everyone involved in the foster and adopted care establishments. Foster and adoptive parents I promise you, this book will become your best friend because the child would no longer be a statistic instead he or she becomes a "person".

~ Linda Wattley

# Your Amazing Itty Bitty® Foster & Adoptive Parent Guide

*15 Key Steps to Successfully Connect With Your Foster Or Adopted Teen*

James Poindexter III, CC

Published by Itty Bitty® Publishing
A subsidiary of S & P Productions, Inc.

Copyright © 2017 **James Poindexter III,CC**

All rights reserved. No part of this book may be reproduced or transmitted in any form or by any means, electronic or mechanical, including photocopying, recording or by any information storage and retrieval system, without written permission of the publisher, except for inclusion of brief quotations in a review.

Printed in the United States of America

Itty Bitty Publishing
311 Main Street, Suite D
El Segundo, CA 90245
(310) 640-8885

ISBN: 978-0-9987597-8-4

*This book is dedicated to the National Youth Advocate Program, Brad Risor, Renee Ellenberger, Marvena Twigg, Mubarak Awad, Sensei Ralph Sumlin, Jeffrey Bubb, Robin and Caroline Griffith, my wonderful wife Rawnak Poindexter and my daughter Nevaeh Poindexter.*

*All of you helped turn an abandoned, angry and violent kid who was going nowhere into a World Champion, a College Graduate, a Business Owner, a Husband and a Father. I never thought I could become any of these things.*

*I would not have done this without all of you seeing in me what I did not see in myself and then giving me the time, patience and love (often tough love) it took to push me to reach new heights. From the bottom of my heart, thank you!*

Stop by our Itty Bitty® website to find more interesting entries regarding Foster and Adoptive parenting information.

www.IttyBittyPublishing.com

Or visit **James Poindexter III, CC** at

www.jameshpoindexter.com

## Table of Contents

| | |
|---|---|
| Step 1. | First Impressions Are Important |
| Step 2. | We Need You During The Adjustment Period |
| Step 3. | No Labels Or Hurtful Statements Please |
| Step 4. | Give Us An Outlet |
| Step 5. | Teach Us Life Skills |
| Step 6. | Don't Rub It In Our Face |
| Step 7. | Ways To Discipline |
| Step 8. | Keep A Book Of Success |
| Step 9. | If You Say You'll Do Something, Do It |
| Step 10. | Have An Open Mind |
| Step 11. | Look And Listen And Apply |
| Step 12. | Don't Judge Me Because Of My Behavior |
| Step 13. | If We Argue, I Will Say Mean Things But I Still Need You |
| Step 14. | The Same Key Doesn't Fit Every Lock |
| Step 15. | We Appreciate You, Even If We Don't Say It Immediately |

# Introduction

This book is my way of helping anyone who is trying to connect with a teen in foster care, who may want to adopt or move their teen out of the system into legal guardianship.

Having been in the system for so long, I have a view of it from the inside. I am not a doctor or therapist or anything like that. I am someone who lived through it and that is far more valuable than studying it in textbooks and then talking as if you really know what's happening.

Most of those people know statistics. I know real life details. What I write here is my and other actual foster kids' opinions according to what we experienced. Everyone is different so these tips will work on some, but not others.

I am confident that if nothing else this book will teach you a few tips to make life with your teen easier and more fun!

*A Word From Your New Kid*

# Step 1
## First Impressions Are Important

From the moment we get out of the social workers car and are entering your property we are analyzing everything. It's very important to welcome us into your home in a warm friendly way. Once we enter your house and see you it is no different than when you meet someone for the first time. We are going to be moving into your house to stay so we are have to get a feel for you and your environment. So what is the best way to welcome us?

1. Please have an open mind. Don't judge us on our situation or appearance.
2. Be very warm with your greeting. Please don't make a huge deal about it though. We already feel awkward as it is.
3. During the introduction, tell us what you expect us to call you from the beginning so there is no confusion.
4. Give us a tour, show us where we will be staying and then please give us some space. This is a very stressful time.
5. Understand that we have lost our parents and all our friends so we may be very quiet for a little while.

## Our First Real Conversation

When we finally have our talk:

- The hardest part comes now, that awkward time of adjustment. Communication from you is key here. We need to know what you expect of us and how we can dissipate the awkward period as soon as possible
- Every kid is different so just be very patient and speak clearly.
- Don't act any different to us than you would any other time with anyone else. We want to feel as normal as possible.

# Step 2
## We Need You During The Adjustment Period

The next several months after we join your family will be awkward for all of us as we get to know each other. As teens, we are already changing inside and now due to our situation we are changing homes too. Losing everyone we have ever known is hard and we will show that stress in different ways according to our particular situation. No matter what happens though, we still need you to be there for us. Even if we act like we want to be alone we know we need support. Don't let our tough talk fool you. You are a big deal to us.

1. Being open to talk at any time is always a good thing for us. With emotions going all over the place, don't be surprised if we are happy one moment, sad the next and upset as well. Just be ready with encouraging words.
2. If we have moved often, it will take longer for us to trust you. Please don't expect us to be ourselves right away. The more placements we've had, the easier it is for us to keep our distance because we lose trust in people every time. We feel like we don't belong.
3. We want to feel like we are the same as everyone else. Please don't treat us any different.

## House Do's And Don'ts

- Let us watch how your house functions at first before expecting us to be part of it.
- We don't know anything about you or how you do things. Let us join when we are ready. We will.
- Also please don't show favoritism if you have your own children. This is one of the most common situations that cause conflict between foster kids and their families.

# Step 3
## No Labels Or Hurtful Statements – Please!

Labels hurt and are not necessary. There are also many statements that can be considered low blows and extremely sensitive to us. Each kid is different, but the list I have applies to most of us. Please don't say or do these things to us.

1. DO NOT CALL US FOSTER KIDS!!! We are "kids in foster care." Foster care is our situation, not our label. Ask us what we would like to be called for all situations. We don't want to be isolated or feel more different than we already do.
2. Most of us have parents. Some of us want to return to them and some of us still visit them. Do not expect us to call you mom and dad. There is a chance that our parents abused us so it hurts to say the words. We are not trying to offend you by not calling you that.
3. Tell your immediate biological family not to question us about how we got here. There is never a positive reason for a kid to end up in foster care or adoption which means we have to relive that negative situation over again every time someone asks. If we want to tell then we will.

## Very Important Tips To Avoid Trust Issues

- Please do not say that you "know what we are going through" or "you understand our pain." You DO NOT understand anything about our situation. You got our file and read it and that's all. The reason you are allowed to be a foster or adoptive parent in the first place is because you have a stable situation. Your life is far more normal than ours could ever be. When you make those statements it makes us put up a wall and see you as fake.
- Be mindful of what you say behind closed doors. Walls are thin and we probably aren't sleeping well at first. We can hear you. If you had a rough day with us and need to vent, do it on a different floor or out of our earshot.

# Step 4
## Give Us An Outlet

There is nothing worse for us than moving into someone's home and then having nothing to do.

1. Give us a tour of the neighborhood so we can see what's around us.
2. Ask us what we would like to do as a hobby or sport.
3. Make sure we are involved in all family activities. This helps with feeling like we belong and helps pull us out of our shell.
4. We may not participate the first time but don't worry, we will.

## Activities That Create Positive Results

- Martial Arts (discipline, humility, confidence builder).
- R.O.T.C (discipline, humility, teamwork builder).
- Boxing (discipline for diet and exercise, confidence builder).
- Chess (strategic thinking, intelligence builder).
- School Sports (social skills builder, teamwork).
- Arts and Crafts (creativity builder).
- Music Lessons (intelligence builder, discipline).
- Mechanics (independent life skill).
- Cooking Lessons (independent life skill).
- Family Chores (independent life skill).

# Step 5
## Teach Us Life Skills

While we are living with you, we will need to learn skills we can take with us once we become independent.

1. Most kids in the system aren't taught the necessary skills to be independent; especially if we lived in a lot of residential group homes.
2. Some states have an independent living program, but most still don't so we will be looking to you to teach us what we need to know to make the transition into independence.

## Skills We Need To Learn Before We Are Independent.

- CREDIT!! Teach us about credit.
- Housekeeping skills (cooking, cleaning, laundry, trash).
- Money skills (opening accounts, balancing checkbooks, bills).
- Job skills (resume writing, interviewing, keeping a job).
- How to find deals when shopping (negotiating, researching deals before leaving the house).
- Learning how to be alone.
- How to manage our time correctly.

# Step 6
## Don't Rub It In Our Face

We know you are letting us stay in your home because we don't have anywhere else to go.

1. If we don't do something correctly, reminding us that you gave us a home as a form of discipline only lowers our self-esteem and could make us more resentful.
2. Just because you say certain things to your own kids doesn't mean you can say them to us. They were raised by you. We are here because we have no place to go.
3. We are grateful to have a home. At the same time we are still going to disagree sometimes. When this happens, please don't hold our need of your home over our head.

**Things You Say To Your Biological Kids That May Not Work With Us.**

- "You're grounded" We don't care. We have been through worse and having a home to stay in is fine with us.
- "Do as I say" Doesn't work either. The truth is that most of us don't expect to be in your home long so if you don't connect with us correctly we will do what we want until we leave.
- "I know what's best for you" If you haven't gone through what we have, then we won't believe you when you say this. This is why that initial connection is so key. If we can trust then we will be far more receptive to you. You actually might be right but if the connection between us isn't good we won't care much to listen.

# Step 7
## Ways To Discipline

Disciplining us can be hard because you may not know what triggers us. You must be very careful.

1. Knowing our complete history helps to avoid triggers.
2. Saying "my house my rules" is just another reminder that this is not our house.
3. Please have a point to your discipline. As teens we need to be able to apply your rules to our lives somehow.
4. Saying "because I said so" doesn't accomplish anything.
5. The sandwich method (see page 14) is the best way to give us constructive criticism.

## Sandwich Method Criticism

The sandwich method of constructive criticism is the best to not only communicate with teens but with anyone. Here is how to do it.

- Start with a compliment
- Follow the compliment with the reason you're criticizing
- Finish with a compliment. Ending with a compliment is huge because most people start with a compliment and then say "BUT" and follow it with criticism and end it that way. This is not productive. It erases all the nice things that were said before the "BUT" and ends the talk on a negative note.

Point 5 of this step is huge in developing the connection between parent and youth. An example would be if you tell us to do the laundry but we don't do it.

- Instead of saying "Do it because I said so," tell us "when we are living on our own and if we don't wash our clothes, we're not going to be able to go to work or class or on dates."
- "Ladies don't like guys with dirty clothes."
- This is a perfect way to apply a discipline directly to our lives.

# Step 8
## Keep A Book Of Success

Anytime we accomplish something, keep it in a file, notebook or folder.

1. Keeping a book of success is positive reinforcement towards good behavior.
2. We enjoy looking at our accomplishments since we have been through such hard times and don't have that many to enjoy looking at.
3. There is a file kept on our behavior issues so there should also be a file on the things we have done well.
4. A book of success is something we can keep for a lifetime and show it to others. It's something to be proud of.

**The Book Of Success Can Be Constructed As Follows:**

- Take pictures of good moments and achievements.
- Keep newspaper clippings.
- All certificates should be kept here.
- If there are trophies, take pictures of the trophies and put them in the book.
- Report cards should be kept in the book also.
- Laminate as many of these items as possible to preserve them for a long time.

# Step 9
## If You Say You'll Do Something, Do It

One of the things that harms a good connection between us and the family is when you or someone in your family makes a promise they don't keep or makes plans to do something but doesn't follow through. Following through is important.

1. We have been lied to in most cases by people who were very close to us so if you don't follow through then it's more of the same and we won't trust you.
2. Following through shows us that you are a person of your word which is probably more than we have gotten from anyone else to this point. Our view of you goes up a mile if you keep your word.
3. Keeping promises means you are reliable for the fun things and serious for discipline issues. This will make us listen more because we know you will follow through with everything.

## Common Areas Where Parents Fail to Follow Through

- Being a parent – We don't need parents to be our friends; we need parents to be parents. We need to learn boundaries and feel safe and secure. We need an environment where we can grow. Be our friend once we are grown and independent.
- Not following through with warnings – saying you'll punish us for doing something, but then not following through shows us that you're all bark and no bite
- Promising to take us places, but then getting busy and not following through – It's better to schedule us into a calendar so you can do things with us then not follow through. It's hard enough to adjust to a new family setting with strangers, but then to have to do it alone makes it far harder. We need quality time.

# Step 10
## Have An Open Mind

Having an open mind is usually hard for parents because they have their own expectations of what we should achieve. It's important to remember that we are not you.

1. If we say we want to try an activity that you don't prefer, as long as it's legal and positive let us try it.
2. You never know what we may become so limiting the subjects we want to study, the sport we want to get into or the activity we want to try could be holding us back from discovering something we might really enjoy.
3. Just because you became an accountant (example) doesn't mean we want to become one. Don't automatically put your ideas of what you think we need on us.
4. Support what we want to do. Even if we don't do it very long at least give us a chance at it. This is a huge trust builder.

## Comparing Kids Accomplishments

- If there are other kids in the house, it's not a good idea to bring in someone new and then immediately compare their grades or achievements against each other.
- This breeds competition and the losing side will always have resentment against you and the other kid(s).
- Simply praise each of us for our specific achievements and move on.

# Step 11
## Look, Listen & Apply

When we have a talk we need your undivided attention. After we talk we need you to apply the information discussed in that talk.

1. Our serious talks and family talks should be without phones and with the television off.
2. We have had many people listen, but not apply the things we say. This hurts and makes us feel like we are not being heard.
3. If we are talking and you are looking off in the distance or at your watch or phone, we will take it as you're not interested in what we have to say and we will stop talking since we feel we are being ignored.
4. Sometimes repeating what we say back to us is a good way to let us know you're listening.
5. We don't always need you to come up with a solution. Sometimes we just need you to listen. Let us vent and don't add anything. Be a good listener

## Listening To A Teen

- Far too often when we try to talk to parents, they listen, but then feel they know what's best and want to impose their solution on us instead of applying what we say.
- Parents need to listen with an open mind and not with the "parent alarm" on.

# Step 12
## Don't Judge Me Because Of My Behavior

You may see us act very differently from the way you might act in a situation. You must not judge us for this.

1. Remember that our past is far different from yours so we will react differently than you do.
2. We may only know how to react to a situation in a certain way and if you show us a better way we can change. This is a better model than simply judging.
3. It is possible that you could learn a thing or two from our behavior. Use this as a learning experience instead of judging.
4. We are a product of our environment. We are in your environment now so help us improve.
5. It is always good to put yourself in our shoes. This way you might understand us better.

**Common Types of Judging Foster Teens Face**

- If other teens know we are foster kids they judge us to be bad people. They think we have no home training
- Adults who know we are foster kids tend to be quick to judge that our parents were drug users or beat us.
- Many people think of foster kids as somehow being **"special." We don't have the same experiences so if we are a little slow at learning it doesn't mean we are "special."**

# Step 13
## If We Argue, We Will Say Mean Things But We Still Need You.

During an argument things can get pretty ugly. We will say hurtful things as a defense mechanism. See past it and know that we still need you.

1. We will say, "You're not my mom/dad." Ignore that. It's our way to feel like we have some power. We know we still have to listen
2. "I'm going to tell the social worker." This is another power struggle statement. Don't give up on us over this statement even though it is annoying.
3. "I hate this family." This statement is just us expressing anger because we didn't get something we wanted.
4. We are just like any other teen. We will try to push your buttons and test our limits but that's no different than a biological teen. We will come around. Have patience

**How To Respond When We Say Hurtful Things**

- Stay Calm. It's going to be very hard but we want you to react. Don't give us what we want.
- Maintain control of yourself. Remember that you are the leader and whoever is following you will be watching you the hardest when conflict arises. How you react is an example for your followers on how to react later in the same situation.
- Do not counter a hurtful statement with a hurtful statement. If you do this you have just come down to our level, right where we want you. Don't do it. Don't give us ammo to tell the social workers later.
- Hear us out and then respond. Cutting us off while we are talking will only show us that you're not listening. We are arguing because we are hurt or can't get our way. If you listen to us you can see the real issue and react correctly.

# Step 14
## The Same Key Doesn't Fit Every Lock

This is geared toward parents who have other kids in the house. The way you connect with them probably will not work with us. We are not the same and come from very different circumstances.

1. Do not group us together because we are "kids" and assume the same style of communication works for all of us.
2. One good strategy is asking open-ended questions when you are learning about us. Asking questions about us shows your interest and that's always appreciated.
3. If we are of a different ethnicity, connecting may require something that you are not used to. Time to step out of your comfort zone and learn something new.
4. Another good strategy is doing some recreational activity with us. We tend to talk while we are occupied.
5. Observing what we like is one way to connect. We may not talk a lot but if you watch us you can see what we like and connect from there with a small gift or conversation on those subjects.

## An Example Of A Common Positive Key That Doesn't Fit Us But Fits Most Others

- Holidays for us are usually bad memories and bad occasions.
- Christmas is usually the worst holiday, followed by birthdays.
- We have had to celebrate holidays with strangers for a long time or we didn't celebrate them at all due to our situation.
- Most kids like holidays, but we usually hate them and want to be alone until it's over.
- In school we have to hear about what all the other kids are doing with their families but we are not. This is a bad time for us. Please be patient if we are not celebrating like you are.

# Step 15
## We Appreciate You, Even If We Don't Say So Immediately

As we navigate through the system, we will meet many people. Some people we will see for a long time and some people will come and go from our lives. Parents stay in our minds.

1. Parents teach us lessons we cannot learn from therapists and social workers.
2. We remember the good parents and how much fun we had with them.
3. We also remember the parents with whom we did not have positive experiences.
4. Even if we don't say it to you while we live with you, we appreciate the sacrifice you made to help us.

## For The Loving, Caring Parents

- If you are the last parents we stay with until we age out, stay in our lives. We will need your guidance.
- Know that if you taught us well, those lessons helped us and even if we didn't seem receptive at the time, we learned from you.
- We know the difference between who helps us as their job and who helps us because they really care. If you really cared for us we will eventually try to reconnect with you.

**You've finished. Before you go…**

Tweet/share that you finished this book.

Please star rate this book.

Reviews are solid gold to writers. Please take a few minutes to give us some itty bitty feedback.

## ABOUT THE AUTHOR

James Poindexter III, CC is a former child of foster care who entered the system at the age of 10 after much abuse and being abandoned by his biological parents.

He moved 21 times in the next 5 years before finding a family who would keep him until he aged out of the system. During his time with this family (Robin and Caroline Griffith) and with the help of the National Youth Advocate Program, a top-level foster care agency, and his community, James turned his troubled life completely around.

His parents and NYAP allowed him to enter karate as part of his anger management program. During the next 8 years James, a member of the Fairmont Karate Academy, began to excel. He won 7 National Karate Championships, became a member of the United States Martial Arts Team, won the World Martial Arts Championships and silver-medaled at the Goodwill Games and the World Cup. He also went on to graduate college with 2 degrees and now has his own business, JH Brands, training parents, mentoring youth and speaking professionally about overcoming obstacles and how to think and live like a champion.

James is married to Rawnak Poindexter and has a two year old daughter named Nevaeh. In spite of all the statistics that say otherwise, James has proven that kids in the system can have success.

If you benefitted from this Itty Bitty® Book you might also enjoy…

- **Your Amazing Itty Bitty® Parenting Teens Book** – Gretchen E. Downey

- **Your Amazing Itty Bitty® Communicating With Your Teenager Book** – Christine Alisa

- **Your Amazing Itty Bitty® Veterans Survival Book** – E J Katigbak

Or any of the many other Itty Bitty® books available on line.